HOW TO HEAL YOUR INNER CHILD

5 Life-Changing Steps to Heal The Hurt & Take Back Your Life

Table of Contents

- The wounded child in all of us

- The terrible burden and baggage we choose to lug around

- Our adult struggle to process life in healthy, happy ways

- Change is scary, but liberating

- Sick and tired of being sick and tired?

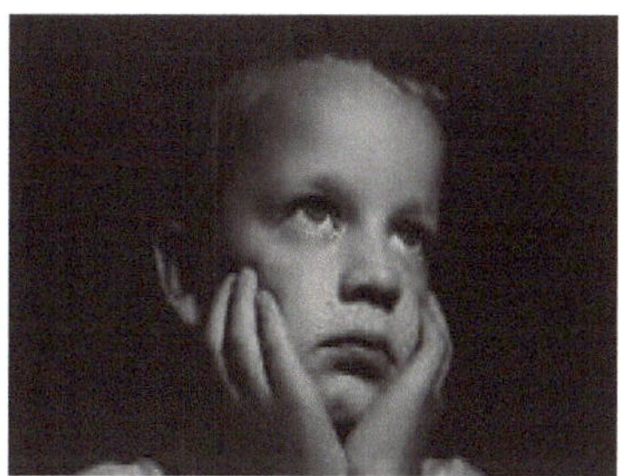

Mitch Before @ Age 55

- 310 lbs.
- *On 15 Medications
- Walking with a cane
- Workaholic
- Addicted to Alcohol & Pills
- Kids & ex-wife hate me
- Few Friends
- Angry & Burnt Out
- Lonely, Irritable, Discontent
- Couch Potato
- Very Sad & Mad

Mitch After @ Age 62

- 199 lbs.
- *Medication Free
- *Workout 5 days/week – totally buff
- Doing what I love with total balance
- Substance Free
- Healed relationships with Family & Friends
- Deep & Loving Friendships at home and at work.
- Free from my past and living in the incredible flow and gifts of my life.
- Meditate & do Yoga, Spin & Cross Fit
- Happy, fulfilled & smiling, relaxed & truly grateful to be alive! At peace with my life & the universe

5 STEPS TO HEALING

1. What is your INNER CHILD & why does IT need healing?

2. What are the benefits & rewards of healing?

3. How do you identify what needs healing in you?

4. Most effective transformational healing strategies

5. How to take back & reclaim you're your life

- 1.Clearly understand the problem & golden opportunity

- 2. Set realistic & achievable goals & expectations for yourself

- 3. Identify & understand your specific issues & how do they manifest in your life?

- 4. Embrace & learn from all the exercises that apply to you

- 5. See your progress & acknowledge it in you heal

- What's hurting you?

- How has it played havoc it your life

- How has this played havoc in your growth & happiness

- Have you had enough pain & dis-ease

- Are you willing to do whatever it takes to breakthrough

- Do you want help? Join our Facebook Group!

- Positive attitudes; willingness, honesty, open-mindedness

- Be prepared to do the "good" work

- Follow all instructions & complete exercises

- Set realistic goals & expectations for yourself.

- But also...

- Have courage; be brave

- Be patient and gentle with yourself

- Lighten-up and have fun

- Work with others of like-mind (support group)

DISCLAIMERS & CAUTIONS

- Disclaimer: there is so much pain to be faced with inner child work.

- These exercises are NOT intended to replace therapy, programs or groups for the inner child or child abuse. If you've gone through child sexual abuse, severe emotional abuse, or have a mental illness, seeking professional help is essential. This course is only meant to be a supplement. Finally,

- if you experience strange or overwhelming emotions while practicing the advice below, please stop immediately. Seek the help of a professional counselor before proceeding.

- Remember that everything takes time. The practices we'll review later are not quick fixes. They're not sparkly wands that will immediately make everything better. But they will give you the basic tools you need for feeling safe, secure, and protected at a core level. I truly hope you find something in this course that will nourish you and your relationship with your inner child.

6 STAGES OF HEALING & GRIEF

Your Journey to a Healthy Adult life

1. Trust

2. Validation

3. Shock & Anger

4. Sadness

5. Remorse

6. Loneliness

WHAT IS YOUR INNER CHILD ?

- Tiny child within needing...

- Nurturing,

- Love,

- Forgiveness,

- Boundaries and structure

- Your childlike aspects: innocence, creativity, joy, wonder, awe, bliss

- Lives within you – part of your soul and who you are today

- Our adult inner child helps us feel excited, invigorated, inspired

- When disconnected, we feel disconnected, lethargic, bored, unhappy, empty

MORE ABOUT YOUR INNER CHILD?

- Part of YOUR psyche

- Retains: innocence, creativity, awe, wonder

- Lives deep within you

THE RISKS OF NOT HEALING?

You're left with...

SHAME, SADNESS, ANGER

THE RISKS OF NOT DEALING?

- Rejection, abandonment, or abuse leads to hiding pain & fear

- Which leads to insanity of self-sabotage in adulthood

- Always chasing our childhood elsewhere

- Never wanting to be reject

- Refuse to let others in – too painful and scary ed or disappointed again

- Refuse to let others in – too painful and scary

 Taught to repress pain? Run away and stay lonely…

 Please parents to win love? End up in codependent relationships

 Must accept and feel your emotions, take care of child within

 Must honor and allow self-care within for both your child and adult

 As adults, very hard on ourselves

 We self-judge, self-loath, self-sabotage

 We see childhood trauma, pain, repressed emotions as separate entity: an "inner child"

 This helps you to be more compassionate towards yourself/others

 Greater the empathy we show others, faster we heal

 WE understand

 Old childhood baggage tough to shake

 Especially true when we were deeply traumatized

 Shine the light on your pain and watch it dissolve

Do You Struggle With Any of These?

- Emotional, physical, sexual abuse

- Depression and anxiety

- Anger management, passive-aggressive behavior

- Low Self-Esteem, -Image, -Worth

- Feelings of abandonment, emotional numbness

- Relationship difficulties, codependency, powerlessness

RESEARCH SHOWS...

It pays off big to be in touch with your inner child

Our parents typically didn't know any better

Need to stop the blame game

From now on, it's an inside job and you have the power

Put the focus on your inner child's unmet needs

The place of our early wounding...

...And most profound healing now!

 We can be brutally hard on ourselves

 We self-judge,-loath,blame

 We have no perspective, no tools, no idea how to change what hurts!

STEP #2

- What are the benefits & rewards of healing?

Greater happiness, optimism, improved creativity, healthier mind, body, soul, stronger friendships, deeper relationships, development of essential life skills: acceptance, forgiveness, vulnerability, compassion, self-love

Repressed memories hold you back from feeling again, building personal power and honoring your self-care needs

Want to like yourself again, feel better about you, feel in control of your life, and maybe even enjoy yourself?

MORE CRAZY GOOD BENEFITS...

Getting in touch with long lost hidden gifts and abilities

Satisfying, Nurturing, life-sustaining relationships

Longer, far better life

Diminished addiction to negative substance/behaviors*

How do you identify what needs healing in you?

4 TYPES OF CHILDHOOD TRAUMA/NEGLECT

Emotional

Psychological

Physical (including sexual),

Spiritual

Take a few moments to breathe and connect with yourself after reading this list.

- Being hit or smacked by your parents/grandparents

- Having an emotionally unavailable parent who withholds affection

- Being "punished" by kicking, shaking, biting, burning, hair pulling, pinching, scratching or "washing out the mouth" with soap

- Being the recipient of molestation, shown pornography, or any other type of sexual contact from a parent, relative or friend

- Being the child of divorce

- Being given inappropriate or burdensome responsibilities (such as caring for your parents)

EXAMPLES OF CHILDHOOD TRAUMA

- Not being fed or provided a safe place to live from your parents

- Abandonment (your caretakers leaving you alone for long periods of time without a babysitter)

- Emotional neglect, i.e. not being nurtured, encouraged or supported

- Being deliberately called names or verbally insulted

- Denigration of your personality

- Destruction of personal belongings

- Excessive demands

- Humiliation

- Car accidents, or other spontaneous traumatic events

- In the deepest part of me, I feel that there's something wrong with me.

- I experience anxiety whenever contemplating doing something new.

- I'm a people-pleaser and tend to lack a strong identity.

- I'm a rebel. I feel more alive when I'm in conflict with others.

- I tend to hoard things and have trouble letting go.

- I feel guilty standing up for myself.

I feel inadequate as a man or woman.

I'm driven to always be a super-achiever.

I consider myself a terrible sinner and I'm afraid of going to hell.

I constantly criticize myself for being inadequate.

I'm rigid and perfectionistic.

I have trouble starting or finishing things.

I'm ashamed of expressing strong emotions such as sadness or anger.

25 SIGNS THAT YOU'RE HURTING INSIDE...

I rarely get mad, but when I do, I become rageful.

I have sex when I don't really want to.

I'm ashamed of my bodily functions.

I spend too much time looking at pornography.

I distrust everyone, including myself.

I am an addict or have beena addicted to something.

I avoid conflict at all costs.

I am afraid of people and tend to avoid them.

I feel more responsible for others than for myself.

I never felt close to one or both of my parents.

My deepest fear is being abandoned and I'll do anything to hold onto a relationship.

I struggle to say "no."

WHAT SHOULD I DO IF I ANSWERED YES?

If you answered YES to ten or more of these statements, working with your inner child should be at the top of your priority list.

If you answered YES to five or more of these statements, you should seriously consider reconnecting with your inner child.

- Pay close attention to these signs. They will help you learn the general extent to which your inner child has been wounded and the level to which you feel unsafe in this world. The more signs you say "yes" to, the more you need to seriously consider inner child work.

- You might feel strong emotions!

- Take your time, go slowly, be gentle

- Neglect from others leads to grudge-holding, blame, anger

- Our parents (and their parents+) were also likely victims of their upbringing

- It's likely not their fault, nor is it yours!

- If it was, it's up to you to heal yourself, not them

Most effective transformational healing strategies

EXERCISES & STRATEGIES TO HEAL

- Reflect on the timeline of your childhood

- Write a letter to your inner child

- Write a letter from your inner child

- Share your pain with a trusted person

- Loving and supportive affirmations

- Do an inner child visualization/meditation

- Be your own protector and nurturer

WRITE THIS DOWN:

- Where are you in your childhood? Infant 0-9mos), Toddler (9mos-3 yrs), Preschool (3-6yrs), School-Aged (6yrs-Puberty)

- At each stage, recall how you felt, what it was like. Did you feel safe, supported, accepted? (Home, School, Neighborhood, Extended Family)

- Record any memories, physical sensations – even if fragmented

- Writing it down honors your inner child's experience and is important

2. WRITE A LETTER TO YOUR INNER CHILD

Become	Become the Wizard or Fairly Godmother
Want	You will want to adopt your inner child
Tell	Tell him/her how much you love them, want to spend time w/ them
Make	Make yourself feel safe, cared for, understood while writing
Download	Download samples letters now https://www.google.com/search?sxsrf=ACYBGNTSikAtWnweqMC-oDdbgkxK2GgvIg%3A1577564827111&source=hp&ei=mroHXriBMs6a_3YmoCQ&q=sample+letter+to+write+to+your+inner+child+pdf-&oq=sample+letters+to+write+to+your+inner+child&gs_l=psy-ab.1.1.33i22i29i30l2.751.6676..10867...0.0..3.518.5206.7j16j4j1j1j1......0....1..gws-wiz.......35i39j0j0i22i30.JJOYZKsfD1g

3. WRITE A LETTER FROM YOUR INNER CHILD

NEXT...

Write yourself a letter from your inner child's perspective

Use your non-dominant hand to get in touch

Give yourself permission to get in-touch with your inner child's deepest feelings

Download sample letters now

4. SHARE YOUR PAIN WITH A TRUSTED PERSON

- Seek out a trusted friend and share and validate your pain

- We need to hold and honor the space for others

- If you want to breakthrough: to heal deeply, profoundly, share it

- Warning: do not share with family members

5. LOVING AND SUPPORTIVE AFFIRMATIONS

- Powerful, safe way to affirm your worthiness, support for your journey

- Repeating affirmations helps rewire the brain from old programming

- Can result in deep, unconscious change at primal level

- Download the file of sample affirmations. Try them all or pick your favorites, but don't skip this exercise https://motivationping.com/inner-child-affirmations/

- Let's try one together now, I'll be here for you!

6. DO AN INNER CHILD VISUALIZATION/MEDITATION

 You'll need +/- 30 minutes or more

 Find quiet, comfortable space

 Sit or lie down

 Imagine with me together that you are about to meet your inner child

Watch these: https://www.youtube.com/watch?v=_aPdpHKdf2M

https://www.youtube.com/watch?v=Mpfl_wAVGBk

https://www.youtube.com/watch?v=Tm9mJUwrLi4

7. BE YOUR OWN PROTECTOR AND NURTURER

Take responsibility for your emotional well-being

Feeling safe most important

You're unsafe if feeling anxiety around others, excessive worry, inability to trust others or yourself, harshly criticize yourself, fearful of trying new things, going to new places, assuming the worst (awfulizing), always feeling on edge

You need to be your own parent here!

- "I love you"

- "I hear you"

- "You deserve this"

- "I'm sorry"

- "I forgive you"

- "Thank you"

- "You did your best"

HOW DO YOU FEEL RIGHT NOW?

- Do you feel raw? Like you've been worked over?

- Are you uncertain what to do with these uncomfortable feelings?

- The results of your buried, often unresolved past can be shocking and difficult

- Talk with a trusted advisor/friend, professional

- Keep doing the work of change!

STEP #5

How to take back & reclaim you're life

- Know you are good and enough

- Stop worrying about what other people think of you

- Step out of the drama in your life

- Build real friendships

- Focus on building a great self-care program

- Grow your spiritual life

- continue to drop the rocks of self-pity, remorse, shame, anger, resentment

- Focus on growth tools like love (self/other), experiences not things, nurturing long-lasting relationships

- Develop positive attitudes, actions, and behaviors

- Practice gratitude

- Become present for your life

 How to Know if you're healing

 Write yourself a letter from your inner child's perspective

 Keep practicing more of a good thing

 You are good. Now it's time to know it for real!

- THE HEALING ACADEMY (url)/facebook group)
- Healing from Toxic Parents
- Happiness Mastery System
- 21-Day Happiness Challenge
- Making Love Work
- Making Life Work
- Spiritual Journey
- Mindfulness & Meditation
- All my e-books

www.ingramcontent.com/pod-product-compliance
Lightning Source LLC
Chambersburg PA
CBHW042000110726
48006CB00004B/947